The ENTP Plan
Invent Yourself, Make Progress and Thrive as the Charming and Visionary ENTP

The Ultimate Guide To The ENTP Personality Type

Use Your Natural Talents and Personality Traits To Succeed
In Your Career, Relationships, and Purpose In Life.

Dan Johnston

Cover Design by Scientist X Designs

www.DreamsAroundTheWorld.com

CONTENTS

WHY YOU SHOULD READ THIS BOOK

Do you know those people for whom everything just seems easy?

Their career or business is always getting better. Their relationships appear happy and fulfilling. They have a satisfying home life, work life and, by damn, never seem to have a complaint in the world. **Let's call these people the "Thrivers".**

Then there are those for whom life feels like a constant upward swim. At work, they feel like they don't belong. Their relationships are either problematic or unsatisfying. To them life has always been a struggle. Let's call them the strugglers.

What's going on here? Are some of us just blessed with good fortune? Is everyone else just cursed with constant struggle?

Don't worry; there are no magical forces at work – just some psychology. It's been my experience that there is only one difference between the Strugglers and the Thrivers.

The Thrivers, by reflection, study, or just dumb luck, have built their lives around their natural personalities. Their work utilizes their strengths while their relationships complement their weaknesses.

A small percentage of the Thrivers came into their lives "naturally". The careers their parents or teachers recommended were the perfect fit for them, or they had a gut feeling that turned out to be right. They met their ideal partner who complemented them perfectly. I believe, however, that this group is the minority.

Most Thrivers have spent years "watching" themselves and reflecting about who they really are. For some this is a natural process, for others (myself included) it's a more deliberate process. We read, studied, questioned and took tests all in the name of self-awareness. We've made it a priority to know and understand ourselves.

Whatever a Thriver learns about themselves, they use to make significant changes in their life. They change careers, end relationships and start new hobbies. They do all this so that one day their life will be fulfilling and have a natural flow to it: a life in which they can thrive.

This book is for Thrivers: Past, present and future.

If you once had your flow but can't seem to find it again, read on.

If you're in your flow and want to keep and improve it, read on.

And if you're one of the beautiful souls struggling but committed to finding your flow and thriving, you're in the right place. Read on.

Today you may feel like a salmon swimming upstream, but this is a temporary state of being. One day soon, you will find yourself evolving. Perhaps into a dolphin, swimming amongst those with whom you belong, free to be yourself, to play and to enjoy life. Maybe you'd rather find your place as a whale - wise and powerful, roaming the oceans and setting your own path, respected and admired by all.

KNOWLEDGE BRINGS AWARENESS AND AWARENESS BRINGS SUCCESS

I'm an entrepreneur as well as a writer. As an entrepreneur, negotiation plays a big part in any success I might have. One of the secrets to being a good negotiator is to always be the one with the most information in the room. The same holds true for decision making in our personal lives.

When it comes to the big things in life, we can't make a good decision if we don't have all the relevant information.

I think most of us understand this on an external level. When we're shopping for a new car, we research our options: the prices, the engines, and the warranties. We find out as much as we can to help make our decision.

Unfortunately, we often forget the most important factor in our decisions: Us.

A Ford Focus is a better economic decision and a more enjoyable drive than a SUV...but that doesn't matter if you're 7 feet tall or have 5 kids who need to be driven to Hockey in the snow.

When it comes to life decisions, such as our work or relationships, who we are is the most important decision factor.

It doesn't matter if all your friends say he is the perfect guy...it only matters if he's perfect for you. It doesn't matter if your family wants you to be a lawyer, a doctor or an accountant...what do you want to do? If you make your decision based on what the outside world says, you won't find the levels of happiness or fulfillment you desire.

In order to make the best decisions for you, you must first know yourself. That is the purpose of this book: To provide the most in-depth information on the INTP personality type available anywhere.

By Reading This Book You Will:

- Improve self-awareness.
- Uncover your natural strengths.

- Understand your weaknesses.
- Discover new career opportunities.
- Learn how to have better relationships.
- Develop a greater understanding of your family, partner and friends.
- Have the knowledge to build your ideal life around your natural personality.
- Have more happiness, health, love, money and all round life success while feeling more focused and fulfilled.

FREE READER-ONLY EXCLUSIVES: WORKBOOK AND BONUSES

When I wrote this book, I set out to create the most *useful* guide available. I know there will always be bigger or more detailed textbooks out there, but how many of them are actually helpful?

To help you get the most from this book I have created a collection of free extras to support you along the way. To download these, simply visit the special section of my website: www.dreamsaroundtheworld.com/thrive

You will be asked to enter your email address so I can send you the "Thriving Bonus Pack". You'll receive:

1. A 5-part mini-course (delivered via email) with tips on how to optimize your life so you can maximize your strengths and thrive.
2. A compatibility chart showing how you are most likely to relate to the other 15 personality types. You'll discover which people are likely to become good friends (or more) and who you should avoid at all costs.
3. A PDF workbook to ramp up the results you'll get from this book. It's formatted to be printed, so you can fill in your answers to the exercises in each chapter as you go.

To download the Thriving Bonus Pack visit:

www.DreamsAroundTheWorld.com/thrive

DISCOVERING THE "INVENTOR": WHO IS AN ENTP?

At this point, I'm going to assume you're an ENTP and reading about yourself, or reading about someone you care about who is an ENTP.

I'm also going to assume you've read some of the basic descriptions online about ENTPs and have bought this book because you want depth and details on how ENTPs can thrive.

So with that, I won't bore you with a drawn out description of ENTPs here. I'll keep it short, and let you get on to the other chapters where we go deeper into specific areas like career and relationships.

ENTPs are visionary, creative and yet pragmatic individuals. Often highly intelligent, ENTPs are responsible for great inventions, philosophies and performances both in modern times and going back through history.

Significant ENTPs from history include Leonardo Da Vinci, Plato and Voltaire. The 21st century can count Barack Obama, Tom Hanks, Robert Downey Jr. and Jon Stewart amongst notable ENTP politicians and performers.

ENTPs possess a powerful combination of social dexterity, wit, intelligence and level-headedness not found in any other type. This may be why the hosts of the 3 most hilarious and intelligent nightly shows, Jon Stewart, Stephen Colbert, and Bill Maher, are all ENTPs.

When fully developed as individuals, ENTPs gravitate towards ideas they can put into practice. Like ENFPs, with whom they share many traits, ENTPs are often comfortable jumping into a project and figuring out the details as they go, and problems as they come up. ENTPs know they are intelligent and capable problem solvers, so why worry about what could go wrong before even getting started? Whatever happens, the ENTP will be able to handle it.

ENTPs are usually laid back and non-judgmental in their interactions with others. They prefer to inform rather than direct, and believe in letting those around them make their own choices. With this said, ENTPs love to debate and are happy playing both sides of an argument. This ability to see, and play, both sides makes them excellent trial lawyers, debaters, and politicians.

When they apply themselves to the right project or idea, ENTPs are capable of overcoming great challenges and achieving great success in their chosen field or venture.

INTRODUCTION TO THIS SERIES

The goal of this series is to provide a clear window into the strengths, weaknesses, opportunities and challenges of each type.

I want you to have every advantage possible in the areas of work, play, relationships, health and finance.

You'll discover new things about yourself and find new ways to tap into your strengths and create a life where you thrive.

This book is part of a series; each one focuses on one type. You will find I write directly to you, although I do not make an assumption as to your personality type or your traits. I will generally refer to the type, aka ENTP, instead of saying "you". Not every trait of a type applies to everyone of that type, and we never want to make any assumptions about who you are or your limitations.

I would recommend beginning with your type to learn most about yourself, but don't stop there. Each book focuses on a particular type and will be valuable for that type, as well as family, friends, bosses and colleagues of that type.

Even before writing these books I found myself doing extensive reading on the types of my brother, parents, friends and even dates. In my business I would research the types of my assistants, employees and potential business partners. I found that learning about myself got me 60% of the way, and the other 40% came from learning about the other people in my life.

If you plan to read up on all the different types I suggest looking at my "Collection" books, which include multiple types all in one book for a reduced price. It'll be easier and a better price for you than buying each individual book.

13

DISCLAIMER

I know this book will serve you in discovering your strengths and building your self-awareness. I have researched and written this book based on years of practical experience including running multiple businesses, talking to dozens of people about their strengths and weaknesses, and applying this knowledge to my own life to discover my strengths and build a business around what I do best. With that said, I must emphasize that I am not a psychologist, psychiatrist or counselor, or in any way qualified to offer medical advice. The information in this book is intended to improve your life but it does not replace professional advice in any way and is not legal, medical or psychiatric advice. So, if you're in a bad place or may be suffering from a mental illness please seek professional help!

INTRODUCTION TO MYERS BRIGGS

I first discovered Myers Briggs about 5 years ago, although I do have some vague memories of taking a career test in High School. I'm sure that test was likely Myers-Briggs, but who really pays attention to those when you're 16?

Myers-Briggs is one of many options in the world of personality profiles and testing. It is arguably the most popular, and in my opinion it is the best place to start because the results provide insight into all aspects of our lives whereas other tests are often very focused on just career.

Myers-Briggs is based on the idea that we are all different. These differences aren't simply a result of conditioning (as some behavioral psychologists used to argue) but rather a difference in how we're wired.

This doesn't mean that we can't build certain traits, or that any traits are 100% natural. Rather, Myers-Briggs is an opportunity to learn which traits come most naturally to you and which areas you may find challenging or need to invest time in developing.

It's also an opportunity to understand the people around us and get to the root of many conflicts. In fact, understanding the different types and how they relate to others could be the most valuable aspect of Myers-Briggs for many people.

THE 16 TYPES AND FOUR GROUPS

Myers-Briggs includes 16 different personality types that are described by a unique series of 4 letters.

At first, the types appear confusing, but they're really quite simple.

Each type is based on one of two modes of being or thinking for each of the four letters.

- E (extrovert) or I (introvert)
- N (intuitive) or S (sensing)
- T (thinking) or F (feeling)
- P (perceiving) or J (judging)

Now, don't pay too much attention to the words tied to each letter because they don't actually offer a great description for the characteristic.

In just a second I'll share my explanation for each letter. Just before this, I want to share an important point to remember: Personality analysis and profiling is a bit of an art, as well as a science. In other words, since people are so diverse, the descriptions and results aren't always black and white. Some people have a strong preference for one mode or the other, but others are closer to the middle. It's natural for all of us to occasionally feel or demonstrate traits of the other types.

What we want to focus on here is your natural way of being and the functions you are strongest in. It is also important to know that you can, and will, develop your secondary (or auxiliary) and third (or tertiary) "functions" over time and with practice. In doing so, you will create a more balanced personality, with less weak spots, and a more diverse set of skills. In fact, the key to overcoming most personality challenges is to develop your weaker functions.

Generally it's said that we grow our primary function in our early years, our secondary in our twenties and thirties, and our third function some time in our thirties and forties. However, this assumes you're not being proactive and reading a book like this one. In your case, there is no reason you can't leap ahead a few decades and strengthen your other functions ahead of schedule.

WHAT THE FOUR LETTERS MEAN

As you know, there are 4 letters that make up your personality type.

At first these letters can be a little confusing, especially since their descriptions aren't the most telling.

Here's how I explain each letter.

For the first letter in your type, you are either an E, or an I.

The E or I describe how we relate with other people and social situations.

Extroverts are drawn to people, groups, and new social situations. They are generally comfortable at parties and in large groups.

Introverts are more reserved. This is not to say Introverts do now enjoy people, they do. Introverts are just happier in smaller groups, and with people they know and trust like friends or family. Keep in mind, this does not mean that Introverts are not capable of mastering social skills if they must. Rather, they will not be drawn to such situations or find the process as exciting or enjoyable as an extrovert would.

"The Deal Breaker": For some people E or I is obvious. For others the line is blurred. This question will make your preference clear: "Does being around new people or groups add to or drain your energy? If you spent an entire day alone would you feel "off" or bad, or would you be just fine?" If you can spend a day or two alone without feeling bad, or if spending a few hours in a group of people leaves you feeling tired, you're an Introvert.

While Extroverts may often steal a lot of the attention in a room, Introverts often have the upper hand. While many Extroverts crave the spotlight, Introverts are able to sit back and calmly observe, learning more about a situation and making their contributions more meaningful and impactful.

On the other hand, Extroverts have many advantages when it comes to first impressions, wide social circles, and the ability to have fun in large groups and make new friends.

ENTPs are Extroverts. This is why ENTPs enjoy being around people and are so socially skilled within groups or when meeting new people.

For the second letter, you are either an N or an S.

This trait describes how we interact with the world.

Those with the intuitive trait (N) tend to be introspective and imaginative. They enjoy theoretical discussions and "big picture" kind of ideas. For an extreme example, imagine a philosophy professor with a stained suit jacket and a terribly messy office.

Of course, this isn't the reality for most Ns. Most intuitive people live a happy, fulfilled life full of new ideas and inspirations…all while managing the day-to-day aspects of their lives at an acceptable level. Ns have an exceptional imagination and ability to form new ideas, tell stories, and inspire those around them.

Those with the Sensor trait are observant and in touch with their immediate environment. They prefer practical, "hands on" information to theory. They prefer facts over ideas. For an extreme example, think of a mechanic or military strategist.

ENTPs have the intuitive trait. This is why they are drawn to ideas and have a great imagination and pull towards what is possible.

Third, you are either a T or an F.

This trait describes how you make decisions and come to conclusions, as well as what role emotions play in our personalities and how we deal with them.

Those with the thinker trait are "tough-minded". They tend to be objective and impersonal with others. This can make them appear uncaring, but they are generally very fair. Those with the thinking trait rely on logic and rational arguments for their decisions. The "T" trait would be common amongst (successful) investors and those who need to make impersonal and objective decisions in their careers.

Those with the feeler trait are personal, friendly and sympathetic with others. Their decisions are often influenced by their emotions or the "people" part of a situation. They are also more sensitive and impacted by their emotions, and less afraid to show their emotions to the outside world. The "F" trait would be common amongst counselors and psychologists.

ENTPs have the thinker trait. This is why ENTPs can be so logical. It is also why ENTPs may have trouble empathizing or connecting with more emotional people.

Lastly, you are either a P or a J.

This trait describes how we organize information in our internal and external worlds. This translates into how we schedule ourselves, stay organized, and evaluate our options.

Perceivers are best described as "Probers" or "Explorers". They look for options, opportunities and alternatives; this means they tend to be more creative, open minded and, well, often have messy bedrooms. They're happy to give one plan a try without all the details, knowing they can adjust or try something else in the future.

Judgers are structured and organized. They tend to be more consistent and scheduled Spreadsheets may be their friends and their rooms will be clean...or at least organized. They prefer concrete plans and closure over openness and possibilities.

You would find more Ps amongst artists and creative groups, whereas professions like accountants and engineers would be almost exclusively Js.

ENTPs have the Perceiving trait. This feeds their creativity and adaptability. It is why they have great imaginations, are able to come up with new ideas, and are happy proceeding with a plan before all the details are worked out.

THE FOUR GROUPS

Since the original creation of the 16 types, Psychologists have recognized 4 distinct groups, each containing 4 types. The 4 types within each group have distinct traits in common based on sharing 2 of the 4 traits.

The 4 types are:

- The Artisans (The SPs)
- The Guardians (The SJs)
- The Idealists (The NFs)

- The Rationals (The NTs)

As an ENTP you are a Rational.

Rationals greatest strength is strategy. They are intellectual in speech, and utilitarian in how they pursue their goals.

They are seekers of knowledge and trust reason and logic over emotions and feelings. They seek to gain as much information as possible and apply this knowledge towards long term plans for achieving their goals.

Not known for their empathy, Rationals are considered tough minded in how they deal with others. The truth is, Rationals strive to be honest and fair in their decision making and how they treat people. So even though they may come off as cold or uncaring, their actual decisions are usually very fair and objective.

The Other 3 Rational Types, Your Cousins, Are:

- The Fieldmarshals and Executives: ENTJs
- The Thinker and Architect: INTPs
- The Strategic Mastermind: INTJs

To learn more about how all the types relate and interact, download the free compatibility chart at:

www.DreamsAroundTheWorld.com/thrive

IN GOOD COMPANY: FAMOUS ENTPS

As an ENTP, you are amongst some very good company. In this chapter you'll find a collection of famous and "successful" people who are either confirmed, or suspected, as being ENTPs.

Do not use this chapter as a guide to what you must do or who you must be like. Rather, use this chapter as a source of inspiration. It is a chance to see what's possible as an ENTP and what great things have been accomplished by those who share a similar makeup to you.

Personally, I have found great value in studying famous people from my own type including reading their autobiographies. Most of us spend the early years of our lives feeling lost and trying to figure out our purpose or how we want to end up. I've found studying those of my type who have found their purpose, and then success, gives me a shortcut to understanding my own potential and the directions my life could go.

FAMOUS ENTPS

Scientists, Writers and Thought Leaders
- Plato
- Leonardo da Vinci
- Richard Feynman (Physicist)
- Voltaire
- Catherine the Great
- Niccolo Machiavelli
- Socrates
- Karl Popper
- Werner Heisenberg

Actors and Performers
- Tom Hanks
- Jon Stewart
- Bill Maher
- Sacha Baron Cohen
- Terry Gilliam
- Hugh Grant
- John Cleese
- Robert Downey Jr.
- Stephen Fry
- Bill Hicks
- Karl Lagerfeld

- Steve Wozniak (Co-founder of Apple with Steve Jobs)
- Edmund Burke
- John Stuart Mill
- Murray Rothbard
- Federico Fellini
- Rowan Atkinson
- Neil Patrick Harris
- Salma Hayek
- Gillian Anderson
- Celine Dion
- Elizabeth Olsen
- Jeremy Clarkson
- Adam Savage
- David Hyde Pierce

Politicians and Leaders
- Newt Gingrich
- Barack Obama (According to some)
- Benjamin Franklin (Inventor and politician)
- Henry Kissinger

Worth Noting: If you haven't yet read on any of the other types you may not notice the distinctions of the famous ENTPs. Compared with other types you may notice that famous ENTPs tend to be very charismatic and downright hilarious individuals. All the funniest talk show hosts on TV, except perhaps Conan, are ENTPs. With that said, many ENTPs achieve great success in fields that don't warrant them fame, but do bring them financial success. More on that in the coming chapters.

GOING DEEPER EXERCISE

Of the famous ENTPs on this list, which are you most familiar with?

_____

_____

_____

_____

_____

What are some common elements you notice? These could be specific personality traits or characteristics. It could also include actions they have taken or tough decisions they have made. For example: Going against the grain or choosing to follow a passion.

_____

_____

_____

_____

_____

25

YOUR SECRET WEAPONS
(Aka your unique strengths)

In my own life I have found no greater success secret than discovering, *and applying*, my strengths.

When we are young we're often taught that we need to be good at many things. For example, schools are based on your average grade and most parents which much prefer their child have a smooth report card of all B+s then two A+s and two C-s.

The real world doesn't reward the well-rounded individual, at least not exceptionally well. Those who receive the greatest rewards are those who focus on their strengths and ignore all else. Think of people like Arnold Schwarzenegger, Steve Jobs and Oprah Winfrey.

Does anyone *really* care if Oprah is bad at math, if Arnold has trouble managing his personal life or if Steve Jobs was a bit of an ass to employees from time to time?

Nope. No one cares because each of these Greats focused on their strengths and created an extraordinary life for themselves.

Oprah (an ENFJ) harnessed her empathy and ability to build trust and bond with people to create incredible interviews and connect with her audience.

Arnold (an INTJ) used his focus, discipline, and strategic thinking to achieve incredible goals in fitness, performing and politics despite being the underdog in almost everything he ever did.

Steve Jobs (an I.S.T.P.) kept his energy focused on his creative and visual strengths. His vision was so clear, and his innovations so impressive, that his social graces didn't matter.

Now as you read on you will discover the unique strengths closely linked to ENTPs. While you read this remember that these are the strengths that come naturally to you, but you still need to develop and fine-tune them if you want to thrive.

AN ENTP'S SECRET WEAPONS

- ENTPs are very "quick". They're able to quickly assess information or situations and come to surprisingly accurate conclusions before anyone else in the room. In fact, except for ENFPs, they are the most gifted type at this.
- Thinking big and spotting opportunities.
- ENTPs are able to quickly connect with other people and develop rapport, making those around them feel comfortable.
- ENTPs can be very charming and often have a great sense of humour that impresses but rarely offends.
- ENTPs' quickness is tied to their perceptiveness and intelligence. As part of these same abilities, they're able to see connections between people, situations and ideas that most others miss. This often leads them to create new ideas.
- ENTPs have exceptional communication skills, both spoken and written, and are excellent debaters. This is one reason they are often referred to as the "Lawyer" type.
- Adaptive and diverse: They are generally good at whatever they take on and can find some level of success in many areas.
- ENTPs are "chill". It's easy to get along with them and they go with the flow, rarely causing problems or disagreements.
- Overall, ENTPs are bright and intelligent.

- ENTPs are very adaptive and can function well in most situations. They're very comfortable with change.
- ENTPs are enthusiastic, happy and optimistic.
- ENTPs can quickly read a room or social situation and adapt so they fit in.
- Thinking of new ways to do things others have missed.
- ENTPs are quick on their feet and can answer a question or rebuttal a joke without hesitation.

Highly Developed ENTPs Will Enjoy Even More Super Powers:

- Being great problem solvers. Many ENTPs have a gift for puzzles and games like chess. Of course, they are often able to apply this same ability to real world problems.
- The ability to understand exactly what another person needs, in that moment, and give it to them. Whatever this is (reassurance, compliments, a laugh), often the other person won't even know they needed it until the ENTP gives it to them.
- An ability to innovate and bring high levels of creativity to performing, writing, music and the arts.

In summary, a developed ENTP can be:

- Insightful
- Creative
- Intelligent
- Logical
- Quick
- Intuitive

- Adaptable
- Creative
- Well Liked
- Social
- Supportive
- Inspiring
- Innovative

Keys To Using Your Strengths as an ENTP

- Develop your thinking and planning ability. Focus on learning how to turn an idea into an action plan...and then execute it.
- Avoid being the "finisher" on projects.
- It's easy to get trapped in your head or your ideas. Start a hobby or activity that involves something physical, such as a sport, outdoor activity or artistic craft. This will help you get out of your head and connect your ideas with the world around you.

In this and future chapters, you will discover "Going Deeper" exercises. These are designed to help you better understand and apply the chapter's content. If you're like me you may want to write your answers down. When you bought this book you also got access to a companion workbook you can print and then fill in with your answers as you go. You can download the workbook for free at:

www.DreamsAroundTheWorld.com/thrive

GOING DEEPER EXERCISE

Of the strengths listed above, which most jump out at you as strengths of your own?

_____

_____

_____

_____

_____

What are 3 strengths listed above that you know you have but are not actively using in your life, at least not as much as you know you should?

_____

_____

_____

_____

_____

How could you apply these strengths more frequently?

_____

_____

_____

_____

_____

YOUR KRYPTONITE

(Aka your potential weaknesses)

You didn't think I was going to stop at your strengths did you? As much as I say *focus on your strengths* it is still important to be aware of your weaknesses, even if it is just so you can more easily ignore them.

Below you will find a list of weaknesses, or challenges, common amongst ENTPs. As with strengths, this is not a definitive list and do not take it as a prescription for how ENTPs have to be.

Sometimes I will see posts in a Facebook group for a specific type where people seem overly proud of their type challenges. I remember one post on an ENFP group making light at how the poster had been unable to tidy their room in 4 days. While it was good for a "we've all been there" chuckle, I did find myself turned off at what a chaotic life this person must have. They have chosen to neither fix their weakness (by developing their self-discipline and follow through) nor embrace it (by hiring a maid). Instead, they have chosen to suffer what they described as 4 days of agony simply trying to clean a room.

So if some of these weaknesses don't really resonate with you, **good**. Ignore them and don't assume you should be weak in that area if you're not. If you do connect with some of the weaknesses, take it as an opportunity to either work to improve that area of yourself, or to accept the weakness and find a solution so you don't have to deal with it.

Many of the ENTPs' challenges tend to revolve around an underdeveloped Thinking function and getting lost in ideas and the external world.

COMMON KRYPTONITE FOR THE ENTP

Before they fully develop their personalities, some ENTPs may:

- Be too focused on opportunities and possibilities, never really making a plan or taking action.
- Put their attention on the details of an opportunity (the potential challenges) and become overwhelmed and therefore never take action.
- Be insensitive to the needs or feelings of others. This often happens with people who need more security or commitment (or reassurances of) than the ENTP is used to giving or needs themselves. It can also happen with those "outside" the ENTP's immediate circle of interest or current focus.
- Be very impatient with less intelligent people, or those who want to take their time pondering.
- Be a sucker for excitement and newness. This can lead them into dangerous situations. This can happen on both the practical level, such as in dark alleyways, and the larger life level, such as dangerous financial situations or entering into a risky business.
- Struggle with personal finances. Part of this is a result of their "perceiving" nature. Another part is a result of their tendency to frequently change careers and thus have an unpredictable income.
- Not like to be controlled or control others. This can lead to problems with bosses or as a boss when their employees need more structure and direction.
- Shy away from confrontation. This can lead to tension building and unresolved issues lingering in their relationships.

- Obsess over details that have no real significance to the big picture.

OVERCOMING YOUR WEAKNESSES

Many of the ENTP's weaknesses share a single root cause. If they do not develop their secondary function, "Introverted Thinking", ENTPs can get lost in their "Extroverted Intuition".

OK, enough psych speak. Basically, ENTPs need to learn to think, process, plan and execute, otherwise they're at risk for becoming the "crazy professor" type who can solve complex worldly problems yet is unable to dress himself or pay his bills on time.

If they develop an ability to plan and execute, the ENTP will find more success both in "the real world" and in the world where their visions and ideas live, because they will be more organized, productive and focused...allowing them to truly advance their ideas and inventions.

Start by learning to develop and then execute even the smallest of plans. This could be a grocery list or a plan for your Saturday. You'll be surprised at how quickly your ability to plan and execute will grow.

Going Deeper Exercise

Of the weaknesses listed above, which 3 do you most recognize in yourself?

What are 3 weaknesses listed above that you know are having a significant negative impact on your success?

How could you reduce the impact these weaknesses have on your life, either by learning to overcome them or eliminating the activities that bring them to the surface?

IDEAL CAREER OPTIONS FOR AN ENTP

If you gave a Myers-Briggs test to a group of a few hundred people from the same profession you would see a very clear pattern.

An Accountant in my martial arts class told me that of 600 Chartered Accountants who took the Myers-Briggs test at his firm, he was one of only 3 people who didn't score the same type.

This happens for two reasons:

1)   Selection Bias: People with the personality type for accounting will tend to do well in related tasks and receive hints that that kind of work is right for them. They may especially enjoy numbers, spreadsheets etc.

2)   Survival Bias: Those with the personality type for accounting are most likely to pass the vigorous tests and internships required to become a Charted Accountant.

We are actually much better at finding the right path for us than we give ourselves credit for. In almost every profession, there is a significantly higher percentage of those "typed" to excel in it than random chance would have.

Yet, many people still slip through the cracks, or spend decades searching for that perfect career before finding it.

This chapter will help you avoid the cracks and stop wasting your precious time. Below you'll find a comprehensive list of careers ENTPs tend to be drawn to and succeed in.

There are many more career options beyond this list that I have seen in other books and intentionally not included here. These include "good" options that an ENTP could easily do and succeed in, but would not be as happy or fulfilled as they would in another profession where they could use their real strengths.

I have included only the options I believe ENTPs have an upper hand in *and* the highest likelihood to find fulfillment and success. There are always other options, but why swim upstream if you don't need to, right?

To be most successful, an ENTP should focus on work that:

- Rewards contribution and revolves around a positive, conflict-free work environment.
- Allows for creative contribution and problem solving.
- Allows the ENTP to explore new ideas and approaches, especially those that will create more efficient systems.
- Is performed within a flexible structure and a laid back environment and gives them enough time, freedom and autonomy to operate spontaneously and at your own pace.
- Takes place in an exciting, high-energy environment where constant change is the norm.
- Includes a variety of people, projects and challenges so the day is filled with fun and excitement.
- Acknowledges and rewards original thought, proficiency and the ability to improvise with credit going to the ENTP for their contributions.
  - ➢ Allows them to be the "Starter" on projects and does not force them to handle the details or finish the work they get started.

> Lets the ENTP spend time with a diverse group of people, including those they admire and respect. Of particular interest to the ENTP is spending time around powerful individuals they aspire to be like and have the opportunity to grow their networks (and own power).

POPULAR PROFESSIONS FOR ENTPs

Marketing, Creative and More

- Playwright
- Philosopher
- Professor
- Creative director
- Public relations specialist
- Internet marketer
- Internet architect
- Copywriter
- Public Speaker
- Comedian
- Radio/TV talk show host
- Producer
- Art director
- Actor
- International marketing
- New business development: information services
- Director: stage, movies
- Columnist, critic, and commentator
- Athletic coach and scout
- Criminalist
- Ballistics expert
- Detective

Business

- Entrepreneur
- Inventor
- Lawyer
- Management consultant
- Venture capitalist
- Literary agent
- Photographer
- Journalist
- Restaurant or bar owner
- Corporate or business trainer
- Management consultant
- University president
- Attorney: litigator
- Sales agent: securities & commodities
- Agent and business manager
- Urban and regional planner
- Human resources recruiter
- Ombudsman
- Hotel and motel manager

Planning, Politics and Development
- Strategic planner
- Personnel systems developer
- Real estate agent
- Real estate developer
- Special projects developer
- Investment broker
- Computer analyst
- Industrial design manager
- Logistics consultant for manufacturing
- Network integration specialist
- Financial planner
- Investment banker
- Urban planner
- Politician
- Political or campaign manager
- Political analyst
- Social scientist

GOING DEEPER EXERCISE

Read through the list above and answer the following questions.

1) Which 5-10 careers jump out at you as something you'd enjoy doing?

_____

_____

_____

_____

_____

2) Thinking back to the sections on strengths, what do you notice about the list of careers? What strengths might contribute to success in these careers?

_____

_____

_____

_____

_____

THRIVING AT WORK

There is an astronomical difference between a job you're good at and a career you love and in which you thrive.

While some people are fine just getting by, people like you and I sure aren't. This section will help you thrive at work.

3 FOUNDATIONS FOR THRIVING AT WORK

1) Be aware of your strengths and weaknesses and be selective of the work you do. Be honest in job interviews about where you excel as well as where you struggle.

2) When in a job, take this same honest approach with your supervisor. Explain that you aren't being lazy; rather you feel you could deliver much more *value* to the company by focusing on your strengths.

3) At least once per week, if not daily, stop for a few minutes and ask yourself if you're working in your strengths or struggling in your weaknesses. Remember, you have unique and valuable gifts...but only if you make the effort to use them and avoid getting trapped in the wrong kind of work.

SECRET WEAPONS AT WORK

When it comes to your work, be sure to tap into these work related strengths for ENTPs:

- Ability to see the big picture and understand the consequences of certain actions or ideas.
- The ability to think outside the box and find new possibilities.

- Excellent communication abilities allow ENTPs to engage others and enroll them into a new project or direction.
- Can engage others and activate their enthusiasm for an idea or project.
- Ability to easily understand others. Can often "read between the lines" where others miss an unspoken point.
- Adaptability. Can quickly change directions.
- Rational and methodical thinking. A developed ENTP will be able to think through a situation and come to the right conclusion about what action to take.
- Impartial thinking: ENTPs are able to take on work that isn't aligned with their values without guilt or reservations. For instance, an ENTP lawyer would have no issues with defending a criminal she knew to be guilty.
- Ability to see the big picture and understand the consequences of certain actions or ideas.
- Independent. Able to jump into a project, take risks, and just do it without much supervision or guidance.
- Broad range of interests and the ability to pick up something new and learn it quickly.
- Great social abilities - ENTPs can get along with everyone they work with and will generally be very popular and well liked.
- Courage to try new things, take risks, and find ways to overcome the obstacles that inevitably come along with something new.
- The ability to handle rejection well and are able to maintain their optimism in the face of a challenging situation or setback.

KRYPTONITE AT WORK

To maximize their success, ENTPs should be aware of some challenges they face at work. ENTPs will not always, but *may:*

- Be impatient with people or organizations they see as incompetent or ineffective. This can play out as the employee feeling smarter than their boss and angry their intelligence and contributions aren't properly rewarded.

- Be impatient with people or organizations they see as inflexible or unimaginative.

- Be disorganized or unscheduled.

- Have trouble prioritizing tasks or planning their work and therefore can be indecisive as to what to do next.

- Promise more than they can actually deliver on or misrepresent their abilities. This isn't intentional; it's just a result of their optimism and enthusiasm.

- Be impatient with those who are less creative than them, or those who tend to "ponder" things before making a decision.

- Lack the discipline to complete tasks or follow through on details.

- Dislike ridged or routine tasks, people or systems.

- Be unrealistic and put too much focus on what "could be possible" and then come up short of their objectives.

- Easily become bored or sidetracked when the exciting part of a project ends or when confronted by repetitive tasks.

45

RICH AND HAPPY RELATIONSHIPS

Whoever said opposites attract never met an ENFP + ISTJ couple.

Sure, you want a partner who complements your strengths and weaknesses, but most of us also want someone who understands us: someone with whom we can express our opinions and ideas and be understood.

In this section we'll start with a discussion on what ENTPs are like in relationships. Then we'll look at the most common personality types ENTPs are happy with. Lastly, we will end with some advice on creating and maintaining successful relationships as an ENTP, and *with* an ENTP.

ENTPs In Relationships

ENTPs are fun, friendly and low-maintenance partners. They are usually in a good mood, upbeat and optimistic about their next idea. They love to talk and will spend a lot of time in their relationships discussing ideas, business opportunities or philosophies.

Their love of debate means ENTPs may start arguments just for the fun of it. For this reason ENTPs should be aware of their partner's "appetitive for arguing" and adjust accordingly if their partner is more sensitive to conflict than they are.

ENTPs' Ideal Matches

A note on compatibility: There is no be all and end all. The information on type compatibility is either based on theory or surveys, neither of which will ever provide a universal rule.

NT (rational) types find the greatest relationship *satisfaction* dating NFs. This is likely because they can share a common way of thinking about the world. Two of the most compatible matches for ENTPs are INFJs and ENFPs.

Ultimately, the two individuals involved, and their desire to grow and work to create an incredible relationship, will have the biggest determination of their success together. The one incompatibility that I've noticed time and time again is between Intuitives (Ns) and Sensors (Ss). I think this is because these two groups have fundamentally different ways of interacting with the world and often have trouble understanding one another.

In my own experience in romantic relationships, friendships, and business partnerships, I (a strong Intuitive – ENFP), have always run into trouble with those who rate highly on the Sensor mode of being.

Beyond that, it's all up in the air. Generally, for organization sake, I would suggest that Ps match with a J. The P will benefit from the J's structure and organization, and the J will benefit from the P's creativity and spontaneity.

TIPS FOR DATING AS AN ENTP

- Avoid dating Sensors. In the short term they will be drawn to your creativity, spontaneity and all round fun attitude, but you will likely have trouble communicating with one another on a higher level or engaging in the intellectual debate you love so much.
- ENTPs can be overly enthusiastic. In the early stages of a relationship avoid making gushy or smothering comments in the moment when you just happen to feel something strong. You may turn some partners off, and you may give other partners unrealistic expectations about how strongly you feel for them.
- ENTPs don't enjoy life's details. Cleaning, organization, scheduling...it's not nearly as appealing

as the next big idea. Consider a partner with strengths in these areas to complement you.

- You're likely pretty low maintenance and you value focused time with your ideas and projects. To avoid conflict you need a confident partner who will give you emotional freedom and time to do your own thing.

TIPS FOR DATING AN ENTP

ENTPs are affectionate, warm and loving partners. ENTPs are honest and loyal: If they commit to a relationship they mean it.

- ENTPs may have trouble expressing their feelings. Try and help them along by providing opportunities to casually discuss feelings or situations without judgement. Show them you care and that you're genuinely interested in their happiness.
- ENTPs are not exceptionally well organized, keen on schedules, or great with finances. If you want to build a life with an ENTP, you must accept this and accept them. Develop systems, hire help, or take responsibility for the details of your life together.
- ENTPs are fun, spontaneous and adventurous. Fighting this instinct of theirs will only cause problems, so just embrace and enjoy it.
- ENTPs enjoy time with their ideas and projects and have a tendency to get "sucked in" to their work (or games for that matter) and temporarily neglect the rest of their life...including their relationships. This can be frustrating as a partner, but your ENTP needs to be given space to do their own thing. This isn't a reflection on you or your relationship.

To learn more about how all the types relate and interact, download the free compatibility chart at:

www.DreamsAroundTheWorld.com/thrive

KEYS TO WEALTH, HEALTH, HAPPINESS AND SUCCESS

I hope this book has provided some insights into how you can succeed in the most important areas of your life.

In this last section, I'd like to share eleven strategies to remember that will help you create a balanced and happy life. If you apply them, these strategies will help you enjoy more wealth, health and happiness in your life.

1. ENTPs must follow their strengths and do work that is aligned with their abilities. Take on work that will reward you for your ability to think big and create strategic plans to be successful. Many ENTPs find success in very lucrative careers such as investment banking and real estate development.

2. Face your fears to overcome your weaknesses. Learn to make plans of action and then execute them. This will only happen by taking action and doing it. At first, this could be very uncomfortable. With practice, you will develop this muscle and it will get easier and easier to execute your ideas.

3. Learn to understand others. You have a unique and wonderful way of looking at the world...but it is one of many, and no more right than any other. Learn to understand how other people see the world and your influence will increase while the amount of conflict in your world decreases.

4. Be accountable and take personal responsibility. It is important to be aware of your weaknesses but do not

use this knowledge as an excuse. Never blame others. When you blame others for your circumstances you give away the power to change them. Take responsibility for your life and give yourself the power to change it.

5. ENTPs really dislike repetitive work so stick to "project based" work such as creating an expansion strategy or plan for battling a new competitor.

    Within this work, try and focus on the big picture aspects of the project. ENTPs are visionaries and, if they have learnt to take action on their ideas, possess an incredible ability to get things started and build momentum. This is a tremendous asset...if someone else is there to hammer out the finer points. Partner with people who enjoy the details and will be happy to help carry your vision from an idea to reality.

6. Develop your "Thinking" quality. This will allow you to become more objective and disciplined and turn your ideas into reality. One way to do this is to learn from the other NTs in your life. Particularly, spend time studying your cousins who excel at execution: INTJs and ENTJs.

7. Take time to compare your initial dreams, goals or visions with what actually did happen. ENTPs have a wonderfully optimistic outlook on life. Unfortunately, this outlook lends itself to setting "pie in the sky" goals with unrealistic timeframes.

    You'll never hear me bashing goals for being "unrealistic"...without unrealistic goals we wouldn't have light bulbs, planes or phones; the trouble comes when the goal's difficulty is not matched by commitment or a plan of execution, and so it never actually materializes.

Developing an accurate perception of how long things really take will help you set and achieve goals and make real progress.

8. Plan and schedule time to be around people. When alone for too long, ENTPs can lose their energy, creativity, and zest for life.

9. Make time to spend with people and allow your mind to relax...often it is during this "down time" that the best ideas come about.

10. It's easy to get trapped in your head or your ideas. Start a hobby or activity that involves something physical, such as a sport, outdoor activity, or artistic craft. This will help you get out of your head and connect your ideas with the world around you.

11. ENTPs love intellectual games. Games like Chess and Dominate Game (Risk®) come to mind. Be careful of overindulging in these seemingly harmless games. For the ENTP personality they are very enjoyable, and therefore can become highly addictive. While enjoyable in the moment, spending hours on these games will pull you away from the long-term pursuits that will bring you true and lasting pleasure.

PRACTICAL SOLUTIONS TO COMMON CHALLENGES

There is an old fashioned attitude that tells us to just tough it up, overcome our weaknesses and do everything.

This is stupid.

If you're an exceptional painter you should spend your time painting and leave the toilet cleaning to someone else. If you struggle with negotiation there is nothing wrong with asking a friend or partner to come along and offer support.

The more you allow yourself to offload the tasks and responsibilities you don't enjoy the more success you will experience. Here are a few practical ideas for making the most of your strengths while avoiding your weaknesses.

Hire Help With:

- Accounting
- Cleaning
- Laundry
- Planning Travel
- Organization
- Scheduling
- Life Planning (such as a coach)
- Implementation (someone to initiate action, and help with the details of turning your ideas into reality).
- Business Planning

QUOTES FOR THE ENJOYMENT OF ENTPS ONLY

To end with I've included a collection of fun, inspiring and relatable quotes for ENTPs. Many are from ENTPs (real and fictional), others are simply enjoyable for ENTPs.

Far greater is the glory of the virtue of mortals than that of their riches. How many emperors and how many princes have lived and died and no record of them remains, and they only sought to gain dominions and riches in order that their fame might be ever-lasting. ... Do you not see that wealth in itself confers no honor on him who amasses it, which shall last when he is dead, as does knowledge - knowledge which shall always bear witness like a clarion to its creator, since knowledge is the daughter of its creator, and not the stepdaughter, like wealth.

Leonardo da Vinci

I was as happy doing theater in New York for little or no money as I am now doing television for more money. The happiness, I guess, comes out of it being a good job. The success has to do with the fact that it's a good job that will continue.

David Hyde Pierce

The hardest thing to find in life is balance - especially, the more success you have, the more you look to the other side of the gate.

Celine Dion

The true Enlightenment thinker, the true rationalist, never wants to talk anyone into anything. No, he does not even want to convince; all the time he is aware that he may be wrong. Above all, he values the intellectual independence of others too highly to want to convince them in important matters. He would much rather invite contradiction, preferably in the form of rational and disciplined criticism. He seeks not to convince but to arouse - to challenge others to form free opinions.

Karl Popper

A son could bear complacently the death of his father while the loss of his inheritance might drive him to despair.

Niccolo Machiavelli

You just have to keep trying to do good work, and hope that it leads to more good work. I want to look back on my career and be proud of the work, and be proud that I tried everything. Yes, I want to look back and know that I was terrible at a variety of things.

Jon Stewart

What defines a relationship is the work that's involved to maintain it, and it's constantly changing.

Neil Patrick HARRIS

Men of lofty genius when they are doing the least work are most active.

Leonardo da Vinci

All the best things that I did at Apple came from ... not having done it before, ever. Every single thing that we came out with that was really great, I'd never once done that thing in my life.

Steve Wozniak

You cannot look up at the night sky on the Planet Earth and not wonder what it's like to be up there amongst the stars. And I always look up at the moon and see it as the single most romantic place within the cosmos.

Tom Hanks

I wanted more than ever to gain the affection of everyone in general, great and small. No one was neglected by me, and I made it a rule to believe that I needed everyone and as a result to act in such a way as to win their goodwill, in which I succeeded.

Catherine the Great

Attention to health is life's greatest hindrance.

Plato

Acting still rings my bell as much as it did in high school. Plus, I can now indulge my interests as a producer as well. My work is more fun than fun but, best of all, it's still very scary. You are always walking some kind of high wire.

Tom Hanks

I think life changes every year. This is just a little more comfortable.

Robert Downey Jr.

The man who makes everything that leads to happiness depends upon himself, and not upon other men, has adopted the very best plan for living happily. This is the man of moderation, the man of manly character and wisdom.

Plato

SUGGESTIONS AND FEEDBACK

Like the field of Psychology, this book will always be growing and improving.

If there's something about this book you didn't like, or there is a point you disagreed with, I'd love to hear from you. Perhaps I missed something in my research.

As well, if you're an "experienced" ENTP and you'd like to add your personal story, insight, wisdom or advice to upcoming editions, my readers and I would love to hear from you.

To contribute in any way, you can email me at: dan@dreamsaroundtheworld.com.

Books In The Thrive Personality Type Series

The ENFP Superhero : Harness your gifts, Inspire others and Thrive as an ENFP

Or just visit Amazon and search for "ENFP". Then look for the book by Dan Johnston.

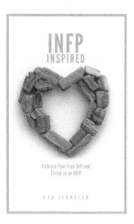

INFP Inspired: Embrace your true self and thrive as an INFP

Or just visit Amazon and search for "INFP". Then look for the book by Dan Johnston.

ENFJ on fire: Utilize your gifts, Change the world and thrive as an ENFJ

Or just visit Amazon and search for "ENFJ". Then look for the book by Dan Johnston.

INFJ, Heart, Mind and Spirit: A Guide to thriving as an INFJ

Or just visit Amazon and search for "INFJ". Then look for the book by Dan Johnston.

The Well Rounded ENTJ: Find more harmony, Improve relationships and thrive as a natural leader

Or just visit Amazon and search for "ENTJ". Then look for the book by Dan Johnston.

INTJ Understood: Harness your strengths and thrive as the unstoppable mastermind

Or just visit Amazon and search for "INTJ". Then look for the book by Dan Johnston.

The ENTP Plan: Invent yourself, make progress and thrive as the charming and visionary ENTP

Or just visit Amazon and search for "ENTP". Then look for the book by Dan Johnston.

INTP: Utilize your strengths, solve life's problems and thrive as the genius thinker type INTP

Or just visit Amazon and search for "INTP". Then look for the book by Dan Johnston.

Thrive Series Collections

The Idealists: Learning To Thrive As, and With, ENFPs, INFPs, ENFJs and INFJs (A Collection Of Four Books From The Thrive Series)

The Rationals: Learning To Thrive As, and With, The INTJ, ENTJ, INTP and ENTP Personality Types (A Collection of Four Books From The Thrive Series)

About The Author

Dan Johnston is a #1 international best-selling author, speaker, coach, and recognized expert in the fields of confidence, psychology and personal transformation. As a coach, one of his specialties is helping clients discover their natural talents, apply them to their true purpose and create a plan of action to live the life of their dreams.

Dan publishes new videos weekly on his YouTube Channel. Here you will hundreds of videos on psychology and personality type.

This is the best place to catch Dan's latest content:
www.YouTube.com/DreamsAroundTheWorld/

If you prefer to listen, check our Dan's podcast here:
www.DreamsAroundTheWorld.com/podcast

To learn more about Dan Johnston and his coaching services visit:
www.DreamsAroundTheWorld.com/coaching

For articles, interviews and resources on entrepreneurship, pursuing your passions, travel and creating the life of your dreams, visit Dreams Around The World and subscribe to the "The Life Design Approach":

www.DreamsAroundTheWorld.com

Find more books By Dan Johnston on his Amazon Author Central Pages:
Amazon.com:
http://www.amazon.com/author/danjohnston

Amazon.co.uk:
http://www.amazon.co.uk/-/e/B00E1DO6OS

Never Settle – A Short Article

This is an article I wrote for revolution. It is on a topic near and dear to my heart. I've included it in this book to let you learn a little bit more about me, and hopefully to inspire you to think big and always go after your dreams. Dan.

Never Settle

"That is seriously your life? You are literally living the dream. That's insane."

I've grown to expect this every time I tell someone about my fairy-tale of a life. But trust me, it wasn't always this way.

A lot people put off travel, passions and happiness until some distant future point; be it the sale of their business, a promotion, or retirement. I used to be one of them.

I owned my own business and I worked like a dog with the dream of one day "making it". Then I could make happiness a priority. I sacrificed friendships, health, family and travel opportunities all because I had to work harder for "just a little while longer." I just needed to "make it" and then things would be different. Then I could I finally start enjoying life.

That was until my business imploded and left me completely, and I mean completely, broke. To get it started I needed to co-sign all the business loans and other liabilities, and so when the business failed so did I. Rock bottom occurred. Public failure. Massive financial stress. All that sort of good stuff.

I can actually remember one night when I was terrified my date would show up hungry because so much as grabbing a pizza together would mean I couldn't afford pasta and milk the following week. I now refer to this time of my life as my "Pursuit of Happyness" phase.

But life must go on, right? What was I going to do, marry a government employee, move to Idaho and get a job as an accountant? Not in this lifetime. And for the record, what the hell does "making it" even mean?!

Fast-forward about 10 months and I'm working as a freelancer and still struggling. It's Saturday evening and the weather is just miserable. Dark clouds, drizzling rain, cold enough to be uncomfortable yet not like a romantic Christmas cold you get bundled up for and almost enjoy. I was at home thinking about my situation and suddenly was overcome with emotions. Where was the light at the end of the tunnel? Something has to change or I'm not going to make it.

I knew I needed to make a serious change in my life because I couldn't handle the stress much longer. The clear decision was to "Call It Quits" and move back home for a bit. Start applying for jobs, save up a little money, and start rebuilding my life.

Lucky for me the windows were fogged that night and I wasn't seeing clearly. Fuelled by half a bottle of red wine and a desire to live true to myself and my word, I booked a one-way ticket to Costa Rica.

Two weeks later, with less than a month's living expenses in the bank and no steady income I was off to the airport and I had no idea what awaited me on the other side.

It was a huge risk...and it paid off.

The change of scener reset my emotional clock. The sun beamed energy into my heart and soul. My business grew, like really grew. Four weeks after arriving in Costa Rica, I called my little brother and surprised him with a plane ticket to come visit me the following week. And yes, I could now afford to treat my date to a pepperoni pizza.

This was early 2012. Since then I've lived in 5 countries, heading towards my 6th next week (Barcelona, Spain). I've crossed countless items from my bucket list including driving a Lamborghini on my birthday, speaking Spanish, playing with a baby monkey, learning to surf and driving a Hank Moody inspired Porsche up Highway 101.

When things got hard I had plenty of opportunities to raise the white flag. To retreat. To turn my back on the life I really wanted.

I'm sure you'll have the same opportunities. Ignore them.

Don't ever, ever think going for it, going after what you really want, will be easy.

But it will always, always be worth it.

For More Visit:

www.DreamsAroundTheWorld.com

Exclusive Reader-Only Bonuses:

To help you get the most from this book I have created a collection of free extras to support you along the way.

When you visit the site below you will be able to download a printable workbook to record your reflections and answers to the end of chapter exercises.

You will also receive free enrollment in a Five-Part E-Course on personality psychology delivered by e-mail. The training is packed with tips, strategies, advice and additional resources.

Through the five lessons, you will learn how to implement what you have learnt about your personality type, including:

- How To Learn From Your Mistakes and Gain Experience Fast
- Why You Must, and How You Can, Become The Best In The World
- How to Overcome Your Weak Spots
- How to Put Your Strengths into Action and Achieve Your Highest Potential.
- How To Pay It Forward By Understanding Those Around You and Helping Them Become Their Best Selves

Both are yours free, a special thank you for my readers.

To receive your free companion course and workbook, visit:

www.dreamsaroundtheworld.com/thrive

Made in the USA
Columbia, SC
19 September 2020